Topophilia

a strong sense of place

Topophilia

a strong sense of place

poems

Sarah Jeannine Booth

Topophilia: A Strong Sense of Place
Copyright © 2023 by Sarah Jeannine Booth.

All rights reserved. This book or any portion thereof may not be reproduced or used in any manner whatsoever without the express written permission of the author except for the use of brief quotations in the context of reviews.

ISBN: 978-1-7389360-0-7

Cover art illustration by Morgan Downie.
Book design & layout by Rachel Clift.
rcliftpoetry.com

First printing edition, 2023.

Sarah Jeannine Booth
@sarahjeanninewrites

for James

CONTENTS

Foreword IX

Note from the Author XI

Woods & Wonder 15

Love & Longing 42

Glossary of Plants 84

FOREWORD

By Holly Ruskin

I have had the pleasure of knowing and working with Sarah for a number of years now, in her capacity as Assistant Editor for Print & Digital at my indie press blood moon POETRY. In this position, she has read and edited many manuscripts (including my own!), and I've been so impressed with her eye for detail. As Guest Editor for Issue 4 of our digital journal, she curated a collection of poetry written by women in response to her title 'Und(h)erstory'…a clever play on words that asked poets to not only think about what lies beneath our exterior shells as women but also tie this into the natural world by thinking about 'understory's' literal meaning: a layer of vegetation between the forest canopy and floor; what darkness and treasures to be found.

And this is how I feel about her debut *Topophilia*.
It is a gem of a book to be discovered and will radiate light from your bookshelf.

Sarah's love for nature gently caresses the pages here and is woven through every single poem. In Woods & Wonder - what feels like a love story written for the Earth itself - she talks of never growing tired of her forest in 'dear forest;' in 'spring solace' it's the delicate beauty to be found in Spring and in another the 'loam, leaf and lament' of my favourite season, Autumn.

Later, in Love & Longing, we are brought closer still to Sarah's core and what turns her world beyond the forest. Here I loved reading 'baked goods are my love language' and 'how to turn sorrow into wisdom.' What speaks to me in this chapter is the pure and unfiltered joy this poet brings to her work and the unfettered access she gives us to her world through the rich and varied language in her poetry. Imagery practically leaps from the page, and this book requires nothing from the reader except our gentle, easy gaze upon its words.

I am proud to know Sarah and deeply honoured to have worked with her to bring women's words to light. We share a philosophy centred on the importance of making space in the literary world for all those women whose work would otherwise go unread, buried beneath the dense weight of a patriarchal society. It brings me so much pleasure to read her work, write about it and recommend it precisely because I know it comes from a place of profound love and meaning for her.

So. Take *Topophilia* outside as Spring crests your horizon. Lie with it as your trees make waves overhead. Look up from the page every now and then (if you can!) and draw in the wonder of what surrounds you. Then, turn back to these words and breathe them in on a fresh summer breeze.

This is a book for all seasons.

With love,

Holly Ruskin
Editor-in-chief
blood moon POETRY

Note from the Author

I often write outdoors. I can find a forest in almost any direction from my home within ten minutes or less. I have learned so much about myself in the woods. Using poetry to write what I see, hear and touch has been an invaluable lesson in my own humanity, insignificance, and joy.

Topophilia is a strong sense of place. The term was coined by Chinese geographer Yi-Fu Tuan, who found no equivalent in the English language to describe this dear connection between humans and the places we know and love.

I'm not sure where my passion for the natural world came from – I suspect it was set in my spirit on inception, placed within me so that the beauty of creation would always point me to a Creator. Let me tell you, it works. The mysteries of a glistening seashore, forest understory, or craggy mountain path are enough to leave me reverent any day.

I began taking poetry writing seriously as a tool to self-soothe during the dreaded lockdowns and global unknowns of early 2020. There was a particularly special unmarked wood near my home where I'd often walk my golden doodle, pen and notebook in hand, taking my time among the trees. I called it "the Sacred Forest;" most days I never saw anyone else there.

That same year, my husband became convinced that we needed a change. So, we began our exodus from the mainland of British Columbia (where I'd lived all my life) to the endlessly inspiring Vancouver Island. At first, I was unconvinced. Could I really make that leap? Could I find my footing a ferry ride away from all I'd ever known?

The move away from where I'd grown up became a breeze as soon as I discovered the raw, quiet beauty that abounded on my new island home. This solidified something I had only dared to hope – nature is connected; no matter where I am, if I can get out in some green, I'm home.

The poems in this collection are a series of love letters. First, to those special places in nature that have captivated my heart - the woods, gardens, and seashores, meadows, lakesides and mountain ranges. Second, to myself as both an act of self-love and introspection. And last, to my husband, James, to whom I dedicate this collection.

It's only been a few years, but I can attest that there is a blessed and necessary tension between learning a new land and remembering where you came from. There is a comfort in exploring familiar flora and fauna in unknown terrain, while recollecting your old haunts and how they shaped you. This is the gift of *Topophilia*.

Lastly, I could not live and love where I am without acknowledging the First Peoples who came before me. Specifically, I live on the stolen lands of the ləkʷəŋən speaking Peoples of the Esquimalt and Songhees Nations. I also want to acknowledge the neighbouring W̱SÁNEĆ Peoples, whose knowledge and relationships with the land continue today.

Sarah Jeannine Booth

P.S. - At the back of this collection, you will find a glossary of plants indigenous to British Columbia, Canada, specifically the lower mainland, near Vancouver and the south part of Vancouver Island. I include each plant's common name and the Latin and SENĆOTEN names (where available.) SENĆOTEN is the language of the W̱SÁNEĆ People. I have included these beloved plants as a reference to the poems in which they appear for those interested in Vancouver Island flora and fauna.

Woods & Wonder

dear forest, part i: spring

i continue to frequent your hallowed trails
your sun spackled glens
your babbling, bird infested twists,
your sweet breezy turns because
i could never grow
tired of you

i'm going back to the earth
to realign my heart with the congruity of green things

grounded, i am rooted by magic and miracles
i love this place; it loves me back
it's never far; this belonging courses through me

i'm unsure how i got here, it doesn't matter
this liminal space is the filament between
my convergence and becoming

topophilia – a strong sense of place

understory

you sit, dormant but alive
waiting to seep, stretch, sow, and grow
you are the green that heals
the dirt that holds
and the humus that nourishes
palms of your hands tipped skyward
soles of your feet planted firm
fed by a sea of sand, silt, loam, and lichen
you unearth what it means to be alive,
become, and then release your splendor
beneath a canopy of trees

this little patch of sun,
caresses my cheek and warms my brow
this cool patch of brambles trails along,
full of flowers then fruits
this sword fern with light green growth
burgeons with freshness,
unfolds new tendrils
this bunch of bleeding hearts
sways in the afternoon breeze,
unbothered by my strolling limbs
this vine maple sprawls skyward – proud
speckled with sky and sunlight
this forest: calm, quiet and untroubled
my daily sanctuary

language barrier

i cling to the bitterness this world brings like roots
with gnarled arms spread toward me
i find strange comfort in earthly unknowing
it's my greatest teacher, this reaching

this subtle informant sneaks wisdom
into the soles of my feet as i wander
this stealth balm heals cracks within
as i walk through fir and cedar

i listen for whispers in secret tongues
this practice tickles my brain
this hidden language, these outstretched limbs
draw me in then back again

all i want to do is write about trees
their moss-covered crags,
their gnarled bark abundance
how can i love something so staunch, so stationary
when i can barely sit still for a moment?
are they sentient? do they speak?

unknowable, ageless, equal parts joy and sorrow
when you place your hand upon a douglas fir trunk
do you feel the static? a warm tingle in your palm?
a calm that starts in your fingertips and flows
liquid amber down your arms, shoulders
chest, straight to your heart?

how about when you wrap your limbs around a mossy oak?
for me, that golden balsam jumps right into my bloodstream
a contact high of happiness
this breath, that leaf, mingled in synchronicity
what can i do with this comfort, this calm
other than immortalize these green memories in verse

the fawn lily in her field
the camas in her meadow
the anna's hummingbird on his craggy branch

these gifts of nature -
no art, no fashion,
no song, no scent can compare.

oh, my heart verily leaps
from my chest in the spring
bound by winter's hope, it clings
spurred by all the mirth it brings

my flourishing soul
is renewed with each bloom
unfurled we make room
for the season's perfume

i have never been more fond
of the gracious new green
and underbrush between
me and chattering birds unseen

there is nothing sweeter
like darling pink lemonade
green sleeves on parade
oh, the wild roses of may!

spring solace

let me write to you
about flowers
those delicate
beauties that come
like subtle
spring sorcerers
set to alleviate
a world holding its collective breath

they stave off
the comfortless and cold
like a gulp of mercy
they relent
like a big sigh,
that new life, fanning
the flames of
recompense as the world warms

april 30 2021

i wake up to bird song
rainfall
mist on the hills
outside my bedroom window
"happy 33" the morning says
my pup to snuggle
warm linen bedding
tucked around me
my hard-working man
making coffee downstairs
these are the only gifts
that truly matter

contentment grows in a garden
there is no other thing
wherein a love so ardent
can hide you 'neath its wing

pleasure grows in the dirt
to toil, and dig, and feed
and in the end, convert
the salvation of a seed

freedom's found in a flower
she counts you as her kin
and delights you und' her bower
your joy unmatched therein

in the forest my pulse quickens
as the lung lichen clings to the trunk
of a gnarled garry oak
regal, resolute

in the forest my heart beats
a rhythm as licorice ferns
sway on an old maple branch
an aeolian dance

in the forest my feet connect
to the sacred understory
as the northern flicker flies
i contemplate my place among the trees

i will not settle for contentment
said rose spirea to the bee
give me life reborn
and endless seasons of immortality

i will not settle for remnant joy
said the thistle to the day
give me sweeping sun's lavish warmth
bathe me in your bluet gaze

i will not settle for listless longing
said the raven to the lake
give me quixotic seasons with which
to dream while i'm awake

there is an ecstasy that only comes
from walking in the rain
ushered in by a brumous sky
hazy water falls from the heavens
cleansing, clearing, cold
the tender fir line
hugs your path and baptizes you
tremble under the unimaginable
weight of evergreen glory
despite your sodden hair and clothes
something ethereal settles over you
winsome, welcoming, warm
what is it? you ask the trees
they know - it is the eros of ambulation
rain - like tears - refines you
you're bathed in green once again

life is a sunrise, new each dawn
the morning sky soaks you in peach
pink and periwinkle whisps

the lapping arms of the ocean,
the cleansing quiet of this morning
are all the medicine you need

i haven't made time to stop and ponder
the evergreen in her glory
the snowberry in her flurry of white
the oregon grape no longer ripe

i've been placid and ineffectual
sedentary and unobservant
this does not a successful poet make
but nature, i'm back and listening – speak!

mesmerized by a metallic sea
nothing else can reach me
no rushing thoughts or outstretched fears
everything else is fleeting

just dappled light and supple waves
salted mist upon my face
breaks in clouds where light appears
a rainbow's hazy luminaire

that hopeful riot of colour calms
this place, for me's a healing balm

the wind
this hallowed ablution
rushes through fir trees
reminds me
even when firmly planted
nature has a way of stirring things up

do i lean in or let go?

dear forest, part ii: autumn

solemnly i scour your foliate corridors
i am ruminant; you are full of room
the days are warm
but the rain will come

soon, maple leaves will flit to their deaths
there's an autumnal feel - both sacred and auspicious
paired with the crisp, dry scents of
loam
leaf
and lament

these will cover your dirt in holy communion
then, you will renew in the waning warmth of the sun
and i will dream of dancing on your floor by the
waxing
light of the
ivory moon

Love & Longing

there is something purifying about an inward inventory
the soul longs to be exhumed

the smell of earl grey tea transports me back in time
i'm 21 again in my best friend's flat
in nelson, new zealand, december 2010 – *summer*
the whackiest christmas i've ever had – *hot, BBQ fare*
walking through town (shoes optional!) with blisters
on my toe pads

before lockdowns, health passports and government panic
we roamed free on the south island with zero care
every morning, i'd enjoy this familiar cup
that sweet bergamot aroma, tantalizing my nostrils,
enticing my tastebuds
a heady taste of home on the other side of the world

to this day, i don't know what went wrong between us
everyone always cites irreconcilable   distances
but that doesn't check out when we'd write each other letters
or long facebook messages in our unique hybrid
concoction of english,
with nods to *"angus, thongs, and full-frontal snogging"*

i don't think it was a matter of belonging
to opposite hemispheres
just a bifurcated path in opposite directions
differing opinions on the meaning of bests
yet, a sip of earl grey tea transports me back to christmas 2010
now tinged with penthos; we're no longer friends

baked goods are my love language

it's a good thing that i love to indulge
in both the baking and partaking

i justify my love of sugar, flour, and butter
by multiple weekly walks down a hill to the sea

to catch the sunrise, stretch my limbs,
salute the breaking day

there's so much pressure to be this, do that;
my heart desires some peace

this salt air, that salt in flour
provide a much needed reward

so, i will continue to seek pleasure
in the bottom of a metal bowl, spatula in hand

to find it in the sweet and salty
the soft and doughy

the crisp and crunchy
the crumbly and gooey

in the warmth and wonder of baked goods
made lovingly by me

these silences
hum
adding tingly comfort
when morning comes

this gilded
light
on green branches
drives away night

this pup of mine
sleeps
morning slumber
soft breath creeps

this dawn-y
quiet

this golden
moment

when my soul
exhales

my sister's partner misunderstood
as i relayed some recent family news
"a baby? congratulations!" he said warmly
to my husband and me from across our crepes and cream
no hint of flush or sadness came as i quickly smiled and offered,
"no, no, our cousin and her man"

what does this mean?
have i finally accepted that i may never be a mother?
what does family look like without children of one's own?
well, from my experience, you build trust and love
and vulnerability with those around you,
blood or no

it's hospitality to strangers who become as close as a brother,
kindred moments spent in secret confidence
with a friend who becomes a sister,
days seem fuller, more alive
when you love and live wholeheartedly
with family – chosen or otherwise

for emery

what a numinous marvel - to be born
despite the world and its anxious sorrows
despite the future and its ambiguity

we enter, first into shock
second into bliss
and third, if we're lucky, love

an unexplainable magic
not unlike galaxies, anemones,
or the boulders of the moeraki

why do geese fly in unison so close to the sea?
what is it about the ocean that pulls them down
like a magnet to a mate?

why do we hold our words close to the chest
neglecting to say what we really mean
until perhaps, too late?

fall song after Joy Harjo

it is a bright fall day
uncommonly warm
the morning sun filters
through the changing oak leaves
the distant rumble of motor cars
barreling down the highway
reminds me: we are close to nature
but not that close
even as your skin resembles
the sand at witty's beach
your hair, the unruly auburn
of an arbutus
your eyes, the mottled hazel
of sage and balanced
liquid amber

a thousand autumn leaves
seeking love's belonging

i'm learning to love
the tender parts of me
ones the world can
and cannot see

some days, there is nothing left to give
you plumb the depths & find only pocket lint

you cannot pour from an empty cup, so fill
fill your soul with all the delights you know

all the grace & gusto you possess
rise above the murk & mess - sing your lark's song

spring for joy, harness happiness
even when you're empty

there is good if you peer outside into the world
then look within, no quick results or haphazard fixes

weep (the gift of tears)
then look up

relish the light of the moon
the first rise of morning, gold to blue

look up

how to turn sorrow into wisdom

time begets healing
profundity in mourning
soft sighs heal worn bones

joy is a sunrise
cleansed by pain, fortitude, clarity
now on holy ground

if joy and sorrow can coexist
then the light and dark within me are well met

no fear
no shame
only wonder where wonders never cease
no tension rebirth cannot release

i glow at the gloaming
stars spark, ignite, renew
i go down to the pit
to find myself - worthy, true

'there you are,' i say
finally, it all makes sense
my sins have led me to
a quenching quest for amends

if joy and sorrow can coexist
then the light and dark within me are well met

these woes are blanketed in snow; smothered in powdered ice
stripped bare, the necessities of life always come
time and again, these anxieties prove fruitless
baying at my chest

the body and the mind are unpredictable mysteries
can i meditate or medicate my way out of the dark?
ride it out; find joy
that glimmer of peace assuages my worn heart

why is winter so difficult?
perhaps the world began in the summer
and humans are wired to thrive under a canicular sun
to find solace under the cool shade of an apple tree

while the water boils for my cream earl grey
i stand at my south-facing kitchen window
the afternoon sun streams in, eyes closed
peach luminance beneath my lids, warm rays bathe my cheeks

life feels wintrier than usual
this blessed moment in the diffused daylight
is a clandestine meeting between my weary heart
and the bountiful sun

though the road is steep and bendy
though the days are sweet and salty
though our hearts beat differently
mine points straight to you

think back to when the afternoon sun
kissed the treetops goodbye
when periwinkle peach
and gold-tinged skies
led the blissful march towards the night
and fused our love forever
even though there was a chill
against your chin, remember?

lying nose to nose in an airbnb queen
our starry breath mingled 'tween crisp white sheets
this is bliss - this tender holiday
watch the worries of the past melt away

languid strolls by cliff peaks,
serenaded by sea lion songs
turquoise ocean shines like sapphires
the waves beat on

we steal a kiss or two
our pup between our legs
not to be forgot, our golden girl
for love she softly begs

she needn't ask, we'll gladly give
and coax her in between
our perfect cocoon of happiness
this getaway by the sea

it's the tenderness i'd miss
your spoon left out after
your morning coffee
perfectly within reach for when i make mine

it's your grease-stained palm print
on the gaucho brown
beam by the bathtub
bracing yourself before you hop in

it's your love for our pup
who really does adore you
whole body shakes
as she hears your truck tumble down the drive

it's your kind heart
that i could not do without
(i'm grateful i don't have to)
it's the tenderness, for me

for the past month, i have held your face in my hands and told you:
"you must allow me to say how much i love and appreciate you"

simple words branded on my tongue
after learning of the unfaithfulness of an old flame

to the one he swore to cherish
and their newborn babe (this shook me to my core)

i saw you in a new light, one that always shone in you, yet until now,
my willful commitment to disparity kept me from seeing it

please forgive me – for waiting so long
for standing too close, for my fuzzy perception of your wonderfulness

you are everything to me; i've made it through the fog,
your light, our love, can radiate now

i showered by candlelight this morning
wood and wax light flickered
hot droplets danced off my body,
as i pondered how the dark isn't dark to you,
you are the absence of darkness.
the moment you said, "my darling," i knew –
the light in me was well met in you

ACKNOWLEDGEMENTS

So many beautiful people made this book possible, and I would be remiss not to express my unending gratitude! First, to Rachel Clift for her tireless and positive leadership in curating this book. She took the guesswork out of self-publishing; I recommend working with her if you consider going the self-publishing route. To Morgan Downie, my lovely cover artist, a true pal and a dedicated collaborator. May this be the first of many book covers! Thanks to Claire Thom for your encouraging words and editor's eye. Holly Ruskin, for your beyond-kind foreword and gentle suggestions early on in this process. I greatly appreciate your leadership and your heart. To my mom, Leslee Gawthrop, for spending the most time with me as an editor, fellow wordsmith, and most beloved critic. I attribute my love of language to you - an unending blessing. To my uncle, Daniel Gawthrop, for paving the way as a writer in our family. I look forward to more writerly chats in the future. To Janice D'Souza, for being an early reader and enthusiast! We all need that friend who will read our writing and simply rave about it, quality aside. You are that hype woman for me, so thanks.

To Professor Tim Lilburn at the University of Victoria for introducing me to the word "Topophilia." As writers, we collect and search for the perfect words to describe our feelings; it wasn't until your class, "Writing A Sense of Place," that I found many words I had unknowingly craved. To Pepakiye, for her help with the SENĆOŦEN, I appreciate you! And to Nancy J. Turner and Richard J. Hebda for their beautifully curated book *Saanich Ethnobotany*, a rich resource for South Vancouver Island plant life.

Finally, to James, my loving husband, who inspired many of the poems here. I know I have a true champion in you, one who - while we often speak different languages - is quick to claim the number one fan position when it comes to my poetry. I could not have written this book without you.

Glossary of Plants

Arbutus: *Arbutus menziesii*, ḰEḰEIŁĆ - Arbutus is an evergreen tree with gnarly bark and branches. It can grow to almost 100 ft and prefers coastal sites with plenty of sun. Their leaves are glossy emerald-green; they produce cream flowers in the spring and orange berries in the summer. Arbutus don't lose their leaves but shed their red, paper-like bark yearly, revealing their greenish-grey trunk. This tree is sacred to the W̱SÁNEĆ Peoples of Vancouver Island; if you have ever seen one up close, it's not hard to imagine why. Arbutus grows predominantly in southwestern British Columbia.

Camas: *Camassia quamash*, ḰȽO,EL - Camas are in the lily family. They have pleasant grass-like leaves with long, sturdy stalks. The flowers are purplish blue and star-like, occasionally white. Camas bulbs are edible and were a traditional food source and of deep cultural importance to the W̱SÁNEĆ Peoples. Today, Camas are found in meadows and hillsides around southern Vancouver Island.

Cedar: *Thuja Plicata*, XPAY - Cedar can reach 200 ft. This evergreen has red bark in thick, fibrous strips along the trunk and branches. The boughs are a shiny green and fall around the tree in 'J' shaped swoops. In the fall, some of the greenery turns brown and falls off, but overall, the species remains robust throughout the year. Cedar grows in Vancouver Island's shaded forests but as far north as Alaska.

Douglas Fir: *Pseudotsuga menziesii*, JSAY – Douglas Fir is a quintessential fir tree with spindly needles shaped like a bottlebrush with reddish-grey bark. Their trunks are smooth when young and gnarled when mature. These gentle giants are known to live well over 1,000 years, can stand as high as 200 ft tall, and are a striking 6 ft wide (try hugging a fir that thick, I dare you). Douglas firs grow throughout most of BC and comprise a good chunk of Vancouver Island forests.

Garry Oak: *Quercus garryana,* ĆEN̲ˏÁŁĆ - Garry Oak is a deciduous tree that can grow up to 80 ft tall. Its branches jut haphazardly as they reach for the sky. The leaves are a glossy green and quintessentially oak-leaf-shaped. They turn brown and drop in the fall. Garry Oak only grows in southwest BC, mainly on Vancouver Island and the small gulf islands nearby. Like Arbutus, Garry Oaks love being by the sea; you often see shorter, lichen-covered clusters on the rocky coasts.

Licorice Fern: *Polypodium glycyrrhiza,* T̲ESIP – Licorice fern tastes like, you guessed it, licorice! It grows throughout the year and is a social fern, preferring to grow in clusters, typically on a mossy branch or rock. They don't grow much more than 10 inches long and are a cheery light green on top, while soft green with orange sori on the bottom. They thrive on wet, mossy surfaces in the forests of Vancouver Island.

[Lung] Lichen: *Lobaria Pulmonaria,* SMEXDELES – Unlike common lichen, Lung Lichen takes on a spongy leaf-like look. It is deep green, pocked on top, off-white on the bottom, and grows on the branches of deciduous trees in moist forests. Not only does its texture resemble lung tissue, but it was traditionally used to treat respiratory issues. (Do your own research before consuming any plants.)

Oregon Grape: *Berberis nervosa,* SENIˏIŁĆ – Despite its name, Oregon Grape grows on Vancouver Island, among other regions. It is a jagged shrub with leaves that are a mid-dark green in the summer and turn a rustic red in the winter. They produce beautifully fragrant yellow flowers in the spring and tart berries in the summer. Oregon grape favours shaded forests.

Rose Spirea: *Spiraea douglasii*, **TÁ‚TEŁP** - Rose Spirea is a deciduous shrub that can reach up to 8 ft. It grows in thickets and favours wet bogs and swampy areas. The branches are brown and spindly, growing in a dense network that produces long, pointed leaves. In the spring-summer months, fragrant, fuzzy, dusky-pink blooms grow, attracting important pollinators.

Pacific Bleeding Heart: *Dicentra Formosa* – Pacific Bleeding Heart is a show-stopping perennial that can reach up to 20 inches tall. It grows in BC and as far as California and prefers moist woodlands. The leaves form a visually pleasing pattern, and a drooping stalk showcases cascading heart-shaped flowers (in varying degrees of pink). Note: this is the only plant I couldn't track down the traditional SENĆOTEN name, perhaps because they originate from eastern Asia.

Snowberry: *Symphoricarpos albus*, **PEPKIYOS** - Snowberry is a hearty, inedible deciduous shrub that grows in mid-elevations and prefers moist to dry areas. It is a common ground cover in Vancouver Island forests that can grow over 6 ft. Bristly branches house pleasant oval leaves and small, soft pink/white flowers in the spring, and creamy white berries, even in the winter months (my husband and I call them 'ammo'). These are not for eating, just hucking at your husband.

Thistle: *Cirsium arvense*, **SIYÁSEŁĆ** - Thistle is an herb with a deep taproot system. They can reach up to 6 ft tall and grow in fields, meadows, and along roadsides, sporting prickly stalks, leaves and bracts. The flowers shoot from the top of the plant in a hair-like pattern and range in colours from white to pink to purple. I have Globe Thistles in my garden, which are said to be a prime plant for pollinators.

Vine Maple: *Acer circinatum*, PENÁEŁĆ -Vine maple is a small tree which can grow up to 23 ft. They display expansive bifurcating branches that create a dense network of dappled green leaves in the spring-summer and gold to bright red leaves in the autumn. The leaves are smaller than a typical maple, growing no more than 5 inches wide. Vine maples favour moist forests and sites where crepuscular rays can reach them.

White Fawn Lily: *Erythronium oregonum*, SĆK,ŚEN – The White Fawn Lily has pale green leaves often mottled with dark brown. The Flowers are white (sometimes pink) with yellow-orange at the center. These blooms excel in meadows and rocky woodlands. My husband and I see them on local walks near the sea in the spring.

Wild Rose: *Rosa Nutkana*, K̲EL,K̲E,IŁĆ - Wild rose is a heady, fragrant deciduous shrub that adapts to its environment if it receives lots of sunlight and moister. Another social plant, under the right circumstances, it grows in close thickets and reaches up to 10 ft. Wild rose stalks are thorny, their leaves toothed and oval, culminating at a gentle point. The flowers contain 5 bright pink petals with cheery yellow centers and come out in early spring. In the summer, scarlets bulbous fruits – hips – appear. These beauties grow in well-lit woods and are evocative of that liminal space between spring and summer.

www.ingramcontent.com/pod-product-compliance
Lightning Source LLC
Chambersburg PA
CBHW030313100526
44590CB00012B/626